AMERICAN HEROES

JOHN GLENN

Hooked on Flying

AMERICAN HEROES

JOHN GLENN
Hooked on Flying

SNEED B. COLLARD III

Marshall Cavendish
Benchmark
New York

For my cousin Lisa,
who puts space heroes on the map

Marshall Cavendish Benchmark
99 White Plains Road
Tarrytown, New York 10591
www.marshallcavendish.us

Library of Congress Cataloging-in-Publication Data
Collard, Sneed B.
John Glenn : hooked on flying / by Sneed B. Collard III.
p. cm. — (American heroes)
Summary: "A juvenile biography of John Glenn, American
astronaut"—Provided by publisher.
Includes bibliographical references and index.
ISBN 978-0-7614-3066-7
1. Glenn, John, 1921————Juvenile literature. 2. Legislators—United
States—Biography—Juvenile literature. 3. United States. Congress.
Senate—Biography—Juvenile literature. 4. Astronauts—United
States—Biography—Juvenile literature. I. Title.
E840.8.G54C66 2009
973.92092—dc22
[B]   2008016009

Editor: Joyce Stanton   Art Director: Anahid Hamparian
Publisher: Michelle Bisson   Designer: Anne Scatto
Printed in Malaysia
135642

Images provided by Debbie Needleman, Picture
Researcher, Portsmouth, NH, from the following
sources:
Front cover: Portrait of John Glenn (oil on canvas)
by NAZA, www.naza.com.
Back cover: Earth Observatory/NASA.
Page i: Portrait of John Glenn (detail) by NAZA,
www.naza.com; *page ii:* NASA/Getty Images;
page vi: NASA (#STS095-702-057);
page 1: U.S. Air Force; *pages 3, 6, 9, 13:* John Glenn
Archives, The Ohio State University;
page 5: ©Museum of Flight/CORBIS;
pages 10, 14: U.S. Navy; *page 17:* ©Rykoff Collection/
CORBIS; *pages 19, 24, 27:* Ralph Morse/Time & Life
Pictures/Getty Images; *page 20:* NASA (KSC – 62PC-
0011); *page 23:* ©Smithsonian Institution/CORBIS;
page 29: Gregory Heisler/Time & Life Pictures/Getty
Images; *page 30:* NASA (STS095-328-031);
page 33: Linda Spillers /Associated Press;
page 34: ©Bettmann/CORBIS.

CONTENTS

A view of the open cargo bay of the space shuttle Discovery *during John Glenn's 1998 trip. Earth is far below.*

*"A boy could not have had a more idyllic childhood
than I did," John would later say.*

From an early age, John loved watching the cars, trucks, and trains pass by his house. Both he and his father were also excited by a new invention, the airplane. In the late 1920s, very few people had ever ridden in an airplane. But one day, when John was eight years old, his father drove him to a grassy airfield. A biplane with an open cockpit sat in the field. "You want to go up?" his father asked. John eagerly agreed. As they flew over the Ohio countryside, John loved the feeling of being in the air. "I was hooked on flying after that," he wrote.

Flying got into John's blood during that very first biplane flight with his dad.

John with his high school basketball team.
He is seated in the front row, second boy from the left.

Of course, John couldn't fly just yet. When the Great Depression hit, his family struggled like everyone else, but his parents kept a positive outlook. John shared that outlook. He worked hard in school and found odd jobs to make money. He stayed interested in new inventions. After high school, he entered Muskingum College and thought about a career in chemistry or medicine.

World War II changed all that.

Even before the United States entered the war, the government knew that it needed more airplane pilots. It began a Civilian Pilot Training Program that paid people to learn to fly. Since his first flight with his dad, John had never stopped thinking about airplanes. He jumped at the chance to fly them. By the time the United States entered the war, John had become a top-notch pilot. He joined the navy, married his childhood sweetheart, Annie Castor, and was sent to the South Pacific to fly for the United States Marine Corps.

*Annie and John were married in 1943, just before
he left to fight in World War II.*

In the South Pacific, John flew fifty-nine missions against Japanese forces.

During World War II, John attacked Japanese positions in the Marshall Islands. He learned to fly many different kinds of airplanes. After he returned home, both his father and Annie's father offered him jobs. But John had other ideas. By now, flying and adventure were in his blood for good. John decided to stay in the military. Soon, he and Annie had two children, Dave and Lyn.

But before long, our nation found itself in another war—this time in Korea. For the first time, John began flying jet-propelled planes. Being a fighter pilot was dangerous work, but it was also thrilling. John fought "dogfights" with enemy pilots and shot down three enemy planes. During the two wars, he earned four Distinguished Service Crosses and eighteen Air Medals.

John earned many honors flying fighter jets during the Korean War.

In this test plane, John set a new speed record for flying across the United States. The time: 3 hours, 23 minutes, and 8.4 seconds.

After the Korean War, John became a test pilot. His job was to fly new military airplanes to see how they worked. "Test work was serious business," John wrote. Often, new types of airplanes didn't work perfectly. They crashed, killing the pilots. But John was good at his job—and lucky. More than once, he came close to losing control, but he always managed to land the new jets safely.

Then, an amazing thing happened.

On October 4, 1957, the Soviet Union launched the first satellite into space. It was called *Sputnik*. This launch shocked the United States. The Soviet Union was our enemy, and Americans were concerned. They feared that the Soviets might one day be able to drop bombs on us from space!

The launch of the Soviet satellite Sputnik kicked America's space program into high gear.

The United States quickly began to build up its own space program. We were far behind. Our rockets weren't as powerful as the Soviet rockets, and we hadn't even trained any astronauts. To catch up with the Soviets, President Dwight Eisenhower created NASA—the National Aeronautics and Space Administration. At the end of 1958, NASA made up a list of more than five hundred pilots who might be qualified to be astronauts. After months of screening and testing, NASA chose only seven.

John was one of them.

John was chosen as one of the first seven U.S. astronauts.

With the launch of Friendship 7, *John became the first American to completely orbit Earth.*

America's first effort to put a man in space was called Project Mercury. John would fly the third Mercury mission. He would be catapulted into space inside the *Friendship 7* space capsule. It was a nervous time. Everyone knew the mission could be dangerous. The launch was delayed several times. Finally, on February 20, 1962, John blasted off into space.

It was an unforgettable trip. John became the first American to completely orbit, or circle, our planet in space. Flying one hundred miles above Earth, he watched the lights of cities in Australia. He saw all of Africa pass beneath him. "Man, this is beautiful," he radioed NASA.

Near the end of his first orbit, though, John ran into problems. The automatic steering for the capsule began to malfunction. Then, NASA began to worry that the capsule's heat shield was not attached properly. This thick metal plate would keep the capsule—and John—from burning up as they plunged back through Earth's atmosphere. After making three orbits, *Friendship 7* fell back to Earth. Everyone held their breath. Would John survive, or would he burn up in the atmosphere?

NASA worried that John and his space capsule might burn up during their return to Earth.

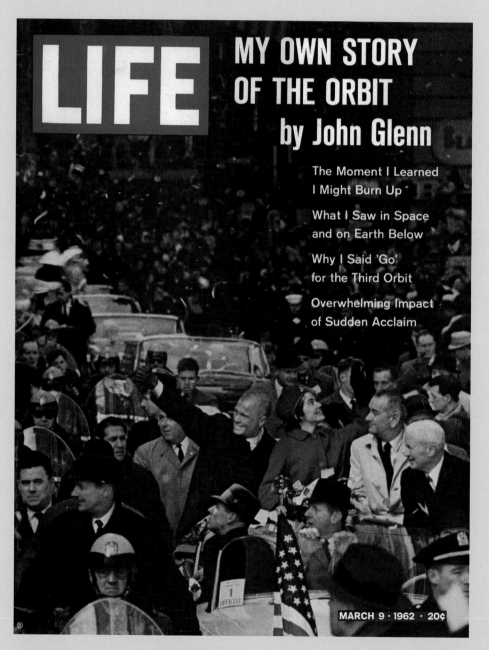

After his first spaceflight, John was welcomed as an American hero.

He survived. His capsule splashed down safely in the Atlantic Ocean and was picked up by a navy destroyer. John became an instant hero. John, Annie, and their two children met with President Kennedy and Vice President Johnson. John spoke to a session of Congress. Parades were held for him. As John later wrote, his flight helped our nation feel "we were back in the [space] race and competing."

John's spaceflight was not the end of his career. In many ways, it was just the beginning. He ran for the U.S. Senate twice before winning in 1974. He served four terms as senator from Ohio. He worked to make our nuclear power plants safer, and tried to make our election system more fair. He also ran for president once, but was unsuccessful. All this time, John never stopped thinking about returning to space.

John was elected to the United States Senate four times.

By the late 1990s, hundreds of people had traveled into space. But John realized that no older people had ever gone there. As his career in politics came to an end, he thought that another spaceflight might help scientists study aging in older people. Other people agreed. John took all the tests that the younger astronauts had to take, and the doctors said he was fit to fly.

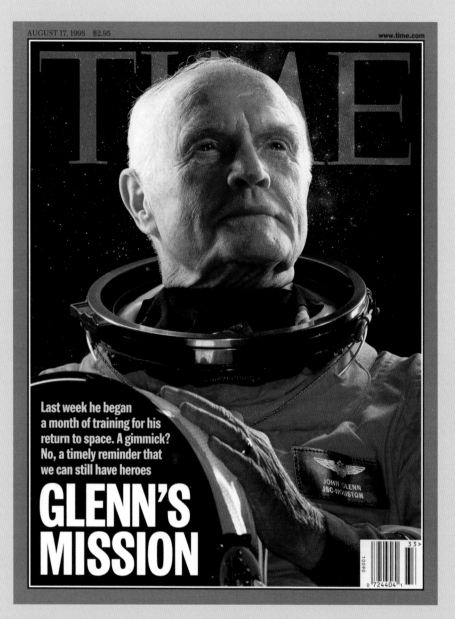

TIME

Last week he began a month of training for his return to space. A gimmick? No, a timely reminder that we can still have heroes

GLENN'S MISSION

JOHN GLENN
JSC-HOUSTON

John became a hero all over again when he was chosen to fly a second space mission.

Before taking off, the crew of the shuttle Discovery *posed for a picture. At seventy-seven, John was the oldest person ever to travel into space.*

John flew into space for the second time on October 29, 1998. His first flight had lasted just under five hours. This time, he spent nine *days* in the space shuttle. He circled our planet 134 times and traveled 3.6 million miles. When he returned to Earth, he once more got a hero's welcome.

Today, John continues to serve his country. He works at the John Glenn Institute for Public Service and Public Policy at Ohio State University. He and Annie speak to audiences around the country. He often likes to remind his fellow Americans about how rewarding public service can be. Life, he says, is not just about getting what we want. It's about giving—giving of ourselves to help make our nation and our planet a better place for everyone.

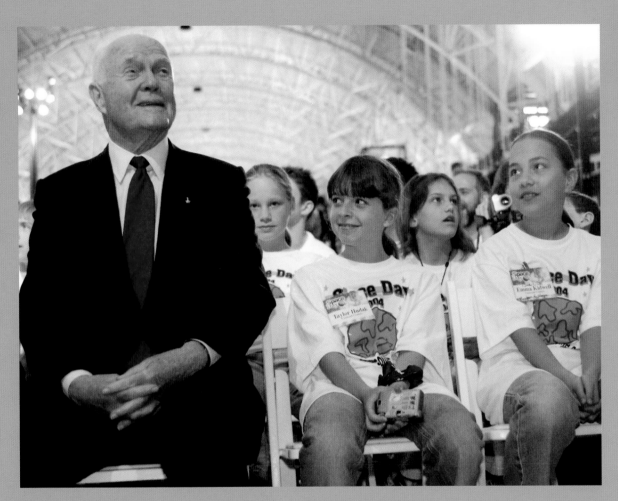

For John, life is about giving to others.

Important Dates

1921 Born on July 18.

1939 Enters Muskingum College.

1941 Learns to fly in the Civilian Pilot Training Program.

1942 Volunteers for the military to fight in World War II.

1943 Marries Annie Castor on April 6.

1944 Begins flying missions for the U.S. Marines against the Japanese in the Marshall Islands.

1953 Begins flying combat missions in Korea.

1959 One of seven pilots chosen to be our nation's first astronauts.

1962 Becomes first American to orbit Earth, February 20.

1974 Elected by the state of Ohio to the United States Senate.

1984 Unsuccessfully runs for president.

1992 Elected to the U.S. Senate for the fourth and final time.

1998 Begins second mission in space aboard the space shuttle *Discovery* on October 29.

Words to Know

astronaut A person who travels into space.

biplane An early style of airplane that had two sets of wings, one above the other.

Congress The branch of our government that helps make laws and run the country; it consists of the House of Representatives and the Senate.

destroyer A kind of large navy fighting ship.

dogfight A battle between two enemy airplanes that is fought at close range.

Great Depression A period in the 1930s when the American economy collapsed and millions of Americans lost their jobs.

idyllic Pleasing and carefree.

malfunction To break, or stop working properly.

NASA (the National Aeronautics and Space Administration) The government agency in charge of the United States space program.

Liftoff: A Photobiography of John Glenn by Don Mitchel. National
 Geographic Society, 2006.

PLACES TO VISIT

The John and Annie Glenn Historic Site
72 West Main Street
P.O. Box 107
New Concord, OH 43762
PHONE: (740) 826-0220
WEB SITE: http://www.johnglennhome.org/index.shtml

Kennedy Space Center (45 minutes east of Orlando)
Kennedy Space Center, FL 32889
PHONE: (329) 449-4444
WEB SITE: http://www.kennedyspacecenter.com/index.asp

Smithsonian National Air and Space Museum
Independence Ave. at 6th Street, SW
Washington, DC 20560
PHONE: (202) 633-1000
WEB SITE: http://www.nasm.si.edu/

INDEX

Page numbers for illustrations are in boldface.

A Note on Quotes

All of the quotes in this book come directly from John Glenn's book, *John Glenn, a Memoir* (Bantam Books, New York, 1999). In most cases, I did not include the entire quote, only the parts of sentences that were important for what I was trying to say. In one case, I added a word in brackets to make the meaning easier to understand. Other than that one word, all of the words in quotes belong to John Glenn.

—Sneed B. Collard III

ABOUT THE AUTHOR

SNEED B. COLLARD III is the author of more than fifty award-winning books for young people, including *Science Warriors*, *Wings*, *Pocket Babies*, and the four-book SCIENCE ADVENTURE series for Benchmark Books. In addition to his writing, Sneed is a popular speaker and presents widely to students, teachers, and the general public. In 2006, he was selected as the *Washington Post*–Children's Book Guild Nonfiction Award winner for his achievements in children's writing. He is also the author of several novels for young adults, including *Dog Sense* and *Flash Point*. To learn more about Sneed, visit his Web site at www.sneedbcollardiii.com.

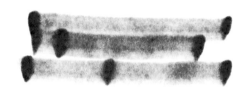